I, _____, IN DEVOTION
BOTH TO THE WILL OF GOD AND TO THIS NATION
THAT HE HAS BLESSED SO RICHLY, DO HEREBY PLEDGE
TO PRAY DAILY FOR THE PRESIDENT OF THE
UNITED STATES AND FOR THE OTHER LEADERS
OF MY NATION AND COMMUNITY.

SIGNATURE: _____

DATE: _____

To register your membership on *The Presidential Prayer Team* and
receive a membership decal and weekly prayer updates, go to
www.presidentialprayerteam.org.

Blessed is the nation whose God is the LORD.

—PSALM 33:12

You will pray to Him, and He will hear you, and you will fulfill your vows.

What you decide will be done, and light will shine on your ways.

—JOB 22:27—28 (NIV)

THE
PRESIDENTIAL
PRAYER TEAM

Prayer Journal

Nashville, Tennesse

We the People *of the United States*

Project editor: Kathy Baker
Associate editor: Michelle Orr

www.thomasnelson.com
www.jcountryman.com

www.presidentialprayerteam.org
www.presidentialprayerkids.org

Design by Kirk DouPonce, interior by Robin Black, UDG|DesignWorks, Sisters, Oregon

Cover art, "Prayer Over the White House" by C. Michael Dudash

ISBN: 1-4041-0079-2

Printed and bound in the United States of America

WHY JOURNAL?

In a busy world, the discipline of journaling might seem out-dated, but it has been used for centuries by some of the most noted and accomplished men and women of history, including many of our presidents and national leaders.

By journaling, leaders like George Washington focused their thoughts and prayers on God and in doing so found the strength and help to serve Him better.

A prayer journal is a valuable tool in many ways. It brings order to your praying by allowing you to keep prayer requests organized in one place. It also makes it easy for you to review how God has answered your prayers, which is a great help in building your faith.

Using a prayer journal doesn't require following a rigid format. You can simply jot down ideas, quotes, meaningful verses, and prayer requests. Some people go for several days without writing anything, while others fill pages on a single day. There is no right or wrong way to use this journal; it simply is intended to be an aid in your prayer life. If you're not sure what to pray about, just look at the short prayers, quotes and Scriptures we've provided to help guide your meditations.

It is our prayer that as you use this journal you will find your prayer life more consistent and more meaningful, and that you will note with joy the answers you receive to your requests.

Whether you read the daily paper, watch or listen to the news, download *The Presidential Prayer Team* updates, or just visit with your friends and family, you can feel the call of God on your heart to pray. As you begin this journey of offering prayers and recording them, you will see the unfolding of God's powerful hand at work—in your home, community, nation, and world.

We the People

www.presidentialprayerteam.org

CONTENTS

★ ★ ★

INTRODUCTION

★ ★ ★

*I*f you write your life, you can capture it. Putting your perspective into words helps you understand and define yourself.

Similarly, if you write your prayers, you can see your spirit. You connect more intensely to God and to whom He has created you to be.

In his prayer journal, George Washington wrote these words:

Direct my thoughts, words and work, wash away my sins in the immaculate blood of the Lamb, and purge my heart by Thy Holy Spirit, from the dross of my natural corruption, that I may with more freedom of mind and liberty will serve Thee, the ever lasting God, in righteousness and holiness this day, and all the days of my life. Increase my faith in the sweet promises of the gospel; give me repentance from dead works; pardon my wanderings, & direct my thoughts unto Thyself, the God of my salvation; teach me how to live in Thy fear, labor in Thy service, and ever to run in the ways of Thy commandments . . .

Washington prayed a bold prayer, a humble prayer, and by committing this prayer to paper, he had a constant reminder of this cry of his heart. The written prayer could encourage and refocus him amid all the challenges he faced.

Leaders today, especially the President of the United States, confront challenges that Washington never could have imagined. Our leaders cannot rely on human wisdom alone as they cope with the myriad complexities of the twenty–first century. They must connect with the holy Source of supernatural wisdom. They must pray.

And our leaders can't carry this burden alone. If we are truly patriotic—and faithful—we must pray, too.

The apostle Paul urged Timothy:

> *I exhort first of all that supplications, prayers, intercessions, and giving of thanks be made for all men, for kings and all who are in authority, that we may lead a quiet and peaceable life in all godliness and reverence. For this is good and acceptable in the sight of God our Savior, who desires all men to be saved and to come to the knowledge of the truth (1 Timothy 2:1–4).*

Does it do any good when we pray for our leaders? Yes! When we talk to God, does He really listen and act? Of course!

James the earthly half–brother of Jesus made this encouraging statement:

> *The effective, fervent prayer of a righteous man avails much (James 5:16).*

The Bible is full of God's promises to listen to us and take care of us, and many of those assurances are included in this book. God loves us, and He wants the best for us. When we pray for our leaders, we show our faithfulness both by obeying God's command and by trusting in His holy wisdom to answer our prayers.

On September 11, 2001 we witnessed a roar of evil, and in the aftermath, investigations revealed how human wisdom failed. Human wisdom inevitably will fail again; holy wisdom is our only hope for security in this life and in the next. Anyone who discourages prayer or who fails to pray is supporting evil, actively or passively. Whether or not you agree with the national administration or policies, our leaders and this nation need to be constantly before the throne of God.

So pray for the President.

Pray for his or her advisors.

Pray that everyone in this nation and throughout the world might *"lead a quiet and peaceable life in all godliness and reverence."*

Pray for holy wisdom and the blessings of God to prevail over darkness.

Thank God for the answers you witness; trust God for the answers you don't see or understand.

Pray. Just pray.

DEAR LORD,

Today as I pray, I particularly ask for the President's heart
to be turned to You in all matters. May purity and light reign there.
May all darkness be driven away.

MY PRAYER FOR THE PRESIDENT

★ ★ ★

_____

_____

_____

_____

_____

_____

_____

_____

_____

Oh, send out Your light and Your truth! _____

Let them lead me; Let them bring me to Your holy hill _____

And to Your tabernacle. _____

—PSALM 43:3 _____

How have you seen prayers for our President and nation answered?

Prayer changes lives and history. Praying for America's officials will empower them to provide inspired, courageous, moral leadership during the domestic and international crises facing all Americans.

—General John Wickham

The President listens to key advisors. Please pray for them too.

The Vice President

DEAR LORD,

May the President heed Your counsel above all else.

May our leader's words and deeds be a pleasing testimony to You.

MY PRAYER FOR THE PRESIDENT

★ ★ ★

With Him are wisdom and strength,

He has counsel and understanding.

—JOB 12:13

How have you seen prayers for our President and nation answered?

_____

_____

_____

_____

We can all pray. We all should pray. We should ask
fulfillment of God's will. We should ask for courage,
wisdom, for the quietness of soul which comes alone to
them who place their lives in His hands.

—President Harry S Truman

_____

The President listens to key advisors. Please pray for them too.

The President's Chief of Staff

_____

_____

_____

_____

DEAR LORD,

I ask for Your favor on the President's health.
May no ailment come near. May our leader be energized
to fulfill the responsibilities of office.

MY PRAYER FOR THE PRESIDENT

★ ★ ★

Beloved, I pray that you may prosper

in all things and be in health,

just as your soul prospers.

—3 JOHN 1:2

HOW HAVE YOU SEEN PRAYERS FOR OUR PRESIDENT
AND NATION ANSWERED?

_____

_____

_____

_____

_____

The Almighty God has blessed our land in many ways.
He has given our people stout hearts and strong arms
with which to strike mighty blows for freedom and
truth. He has given to our country a faith which has
become the hope of all peoples in an anguished world.

—PRESIDENT FRANKLIN D. ROOSEVELT

THE PRESIDENT LISTENS TO KEY ADVISORS.
PLEASE PRAY FOR THEM TOO.

SECRETARY OF HEALTH & HUMAN SERVICES

_____

_____

_____

_____

We the People

DEAR LORD,

Show our President the glory You have prepared for those
who follow You. Give instruction. Open the eyes of our leaders
to true power and purpose.

MY PRAYER FOR THE PRESIDENT

★ ★ ★

For this cause everyone who is godly shall pray to You

In a time when You may be found . . .

I will instruct you and teach you in the way you should go;

I will guide you with My eye.

—PSALM 32:6,8

HOW HAVE YOU SEEN PRAYERS FOR OUR PRESIDENT AND NATION ANSWERED?

★ ★ ★

The men who have guided the destiny
of the United States have found
the strength for their tasks by going to their knees.

—PRESIDENT LYNDON B. JOHNSON

THE PRESIDENT LISTENS TO KEY ADVISORS. PLEASE PRAY FOR THEM TOO.

★ ★ ★

ENVIRONMENTAL PROTECTION AGENCY ADMINISTRATOR

DEAR LORD,

Thank You for our precious freedoms here in the United States of America. Keep us and our leaders always mindful of the blessings we have here. Make the President a good ambassador of freedom and justice throughout the world.

MY PRAYER FOR THE PRESIDENT

★ ★ ★

_____

_____

_____

_____

_____

_____

_____

_____

_____

_____

_____

Stand fast therefore in the liberty by which

Christ has made us free, and

do not be entangled again with a yoke of bondage.

—GALATIANS 5:1

How have you seen prayers for our President and nation answered?

I deem the present occasion sufficiently important and solemn to justify me in expressing to my fellow—citizens a profound reverence for the Christian religion and a thorough conviction that sound morals, religious liberty, and a just sense of religious responsibility are essentially connected with all true and lasting happiness; and to that good Being who has blessed us by the gifts of civil and religious freedom, who watched over and prospered the labors of our fathers and has hitherto preserved to us institutions far exceeding in excellence those of any other people, let us unite in fervently commending every interest of our beloved country in all future time.

—President William Henry Harrison

The President listens to key advisors. Please pray for them too.

U.S. Attorney General

DEAR LORD,

We want our children to grow up in a nation of peace.

We want them to have opportunities to explore their gifts and live up to their

great potential. May our leaders live as godly examples, and may

they make wise decisions that benefit our children.

MY PRAYER FOR THE PRESIDENT

★ ★ ★

Train up a child in the way he should go,

And when he is old he will not depart from it.

—PROVERBS 22:6

How have you seen prayers for our President and nation answered?

In my view, the Christian religion is the most important and one of the first things in which all children, under a free government ought to be instructed . . . No truth is more evident to my mind than that the Christian religion must be the basis of any government intended to secure the rights and privileges of a free people.

—Noah Webster

The President listens to key advisors. Please pray for them too.

Secretary of Education

DEAR LORD,

The President needs my prayers just as this nation needs You. Although I value the logic behind the separation of church and state, I ask, Father, that our leaders' decisions and their lives point people toward You. May opportunities be opened to the truth that only comes from You, and may my neighbors' hearts be made more receptive to receiving Your gospel.

MY PRAYER FOR THE PRESIDENT

★ ★ ★

Hear a just cause, O LORD, Attend to my cry;

give ear to my prayer which is not from deceitful lips.

Let my vindication come from Your presence;

let Your eyes look on the things that are upright.

—PSALM 17:1–2

HOW HAVE YOU SEEN PRAYERS FOR OUR PRESIDENT AND NATION ANSWERED?

_____

_____

_____

_____

Pray the largest prayers. You cannot think a prayer so large that God in answering it, will not wish you had made it larger. Pray not for crutches but wings.

—PHILLIPS BROOKS

THE PRESIDENT LISTENS TO KEY ADVISORS. PLEASE PRAY FOR THEM TOO.

★ ★ ★

U. S. SUPREME COURT JUSTICES

_____

_____

_____

_____

DEAR LORD,

You have blessed this nation so richly with natural resources.
Thank You! Please make our President a good steward of the bounty
You have poured out upon this land.

MY PRAYER FOR THE PRESIDENT

★ ★ ★

_____

_____

_____

_____

_____

_____

_____

_____

_____

The earth is the LORD's, and all its fullness, the world

_____

and those who dwell therein.

—PSALM 24:1

_____

THE PRESIDENTIAL PRAYER TEAM

HOW HAVE YOU SEEN PRAYERS FOR OUR PRESIDENT AND NATION ANSWERED?

★ ★ ★

_____

_____

_____

_____
I pray to heaven to bestow the best of blessings
_____
on this house and all that shall hereafter
_____
inhabit it. May none but honest
_____
and wise men ever rule under this roof.
_____
—PRESIDENT JOHN ADAMS
_____

_____

THE PRESIDENT LISTENS TO KEY ADVISORS. PLEASE PRAY FOR THEM TOO.

★ ★ ★

SECRETARY OF THE INTERIOR

_____

_____

_____

_____

We the People

DEAR LORD,

I thank You for the blessings of Your abundance. Thank You for the fertile fields, grassy ranges, and teeming waters. Please bless our leaders as they, like Joseph in ancient Egypt, manage our food production and distribution.

MY PRAYER FOR THE PRESIDENT

★ ★ ★

For what great nation is there that has God so near to it, as the LORD our God is to us, for whatever reason we may call upon Him?

—DEUTERONOMY 4:7

How have you seen prayers for our President and nation answered?

> *Work as if you were to live 100 years.*
> *Pray as if you were to die tomorrow.*
>
> —Benjamin Franklin

The President listens to key advisors. Please pray for them too.

Secretary of Agriculture

DEAR LORD,

We sing about living in "the land of the free and the home of the brave,"

but sometimes we don't feel so brave or free. Our nation

has enemies who threaten us in so many ways. Father, I ask that

You give our leaders heightened insight into how best to protect us from

terrorists while also protecting our cherished freedoms.

MY PRAYER FOR THE PRESIDENT

★ ★ ★

Then you will call upon Me and go and pray to Me,

and I will listen to you. And you will seek Me and find

Me, when you search for Me with all your heart.

—JEREMIAH 29:12,13

HOW HAVE YOU SEEN PRAYERS FOR OUR PRESIDENT AND NATION ANSWERED?

_____

_____

_____

_____

> *In prayer I am saying in effect, 'My life for yours.'*
> *My time, my energy, my thoughts,*
> *my concentration, my faith—here they are for you.*
> —ELISABETH ELLIOT

_____

_____

THE PRESIDENT LISTENS TO KEY ADVISORS. PLEASE PRAY FOR THEM TOO.

SECRETARY OF HOMELAND DEFENSE

_____

_____

_____

_____

DEAR LORD,

I'm so thankful for the wealth You have provided me. Even during the tough times, the United States consistently is the most powerful economy on earth, and I ask for Your continued blessing on our financial leaders. May the President and all those who administrate the economy make decisions that are shrewd, fair, and merciful.

MY PRAYER FOR THE PRESIDENT

★ ★ ★

_____

_____

_____

_____

_____

_____

_____

_____

"Well done, good and faithful servant; you have been _____

faithful over a few things, I will make you ruler _____

over many things. Enter into the joy of your lord." _____

—MATTHEW 25:23 _____

HOW HAVE YOU SEEN PRAYERS FOR OUR PRESIDENT AND NATION ANSWERED?

I have discovered that the real purpose of prayer is to put God at the center of our attention, and forget our-selves and the impression we are making on others.

—ROSALIND RINKER

THE PRESIDENT LISTENS TO KEY ADVISORS. PLEASE PRAY FOR THEM TOO.

★ ★ ★

SECRETARY OF TREASURY

DEAR LORD,

I can't count the number of times every day that I rely on electricity
to make my surroundings more visible. But You created light
in the first place. You know all the stars in the sky!
Help our leaders to look to You to light their paths today.

MY PRAYER FOR THE PRESIDENT

★ ★ ★

If any of you lacks wisdom, let him ask of God,

who gives to all liberally and

without reproach, and it will be given to him.

—JAMES 1:5

HOW HAVE YOU SEEN PRAYERS FOR OUR PRESIDENT AND NATION ANSWERED?

★ ★ ★

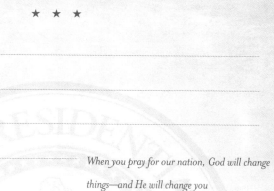

When you pray for our nation, God will change things—and He will change you in a way that will touch your country.

—STORMIE OMARTIAN

THE PRESIDENT LISTENS TO KEY ADVISORS. PLEASE PRAY FOR THEM TOO.

★ ★ ★

SECRETARY OF ENERGY

We the People

DEAR LORD,

We enjoy many freedoms in this country, but we're very aware that freedom
isn't free. Men and women in our armed forces have sacrificed
so much for the United States and for other nations, too. Please help
our President and other leaders properly honor and support those who serve.

MY PRAYER FOR THE PRESIDENT

★ ★ ★

*I thank God, whom I serve with
a pure conscience, as my forefathers did, as without
ceasing I remember you in my prayers.*

—2 TIMOTHY 1:3

How have you seen prayers for our President and nation answered?

★ ★ ★

_____

_____

_____

_____

Remember that God is our only sure trust.

—MARY WASHINGTON,
MOTHER OF GEORGE WASHINGTON

_____

_____

The President listens to key advisors. Please pray for them too.

★ ★ ★

Secretary of Veterans Affairs

_____

_____

_____

_____

DEAR LORD,

From earliest childhood we cry out for things to be "fair," and today we thank You for nurturing this nation where we can publicly demand that our government and employers treat people fairly. Please keep our leaders mindful of the difference between what is merely "fair" and what is actually "holy," and please help us to encourage them always to act in righteousness.

MY PRAYER FOR THE PRESIDENT

★ ★ ★

When the righteous are in authority, the people rejoice;

but when a wicked man rules, the people groan.

—PROVERBS 29:2

How have you seen prayers for our President and nation answered?

★ ★ ★

_____

_____

_____

_____

Beware in your prayers, above everything else, of limiting
God, not only by unbelief, but by fancying that you know
what He can do. Expect unexpected things above all that
we ask or think.

—ANDREW MURRAY

The President listens to key advisors. Please pray for them too.

★ ★ ★

Secretary of Labor

_____

_____

_____

_____

We the People

DEAR LORD,

You alone are holy and wise. We believe and do such foolish things sometimes, and today we acknowledge that we need You to take care of us. Straighten us out, Father. Bring our President and other leaders daily into closer connection with Your will, so that our nation may be blessed.

MY PRAYER FOR THE PRESIDENT

★ ★ ★

_____

_____

_____

_____

_____

_____

_____

_____

_____

[God] heeded their prayer,

because they put their trust in Him.

—1 CHRONICLES 5:20

HOW HAVE YOU SEEN PRAYERS FOR OUR PRESIDENT AND NATION ANSWERED?

★ ★ ★

He who has learned to pray has learned the greatest

----

secret of a holy and happy life.

—WILLIAM LAW

THE PRESIDENT LISTENS TO KEY ADVISORS. PLEASE PRAY FOR THEM TOO.

★ ★ ★

DIRECTOR OF NATIONAL DRUG CONTROL POLICY

DEAR LORD,

Thank You for the blessing of families! I know the President's
decisions affect my own loved ones, and I pray that national leaders will consider
"family values" as more than a buzzword. May the President's
household provide a worthy example of how other families can live, love,
and work together for this nation and Your kingdom.

MY PRAYER FOR THE PRESIDENT

★ ★ ★

_____

_____

_____

_____

_____

_____

Be kindly affectionate to one another

with brotherly love, . . . serving

the Lord, rejoicing in hope, patient in tribulation,

continuing steadfastly in prayer.

—ROMANS 12:10-12

How have you seen prayers for our President and nation answered?

★ ★ ★

_I'm grateful for the prayers of our citizens;
for my family, for the privilege of living in America
and for the freedoms we enjoy._

—President George W. Bush

The President listens to key advisors. Please pray for them too.

★ ★ ★

The First Family

We the People

DEAR LORD,

Give our President a heart for the world, not to dominate it, but to make it a place where Your peace is welcome. We are so blessed in the United States; help our leaders perceive how best to share Your gracious provision to all.

MY PRAYER FOR THE PRESIDENT

★ ★ ★

Oh, give thanks to the LORD for He is good!

For His mercy endures forever.

—PSALM 106:1

How have you seen prayers for our President and nation answered?

Be thankful for the smallest blessing, and you will deserve to receive greater.

—Thomas a Kempis

The President listens to key advisors. Please pray for them too.

Secretary of State

DEAR LORD,

In all times may our leaders look to You, but especially in times of trial and uncertainty I pray that they will seek Your guidance. Give them discernment in knowing good and evil, and give them strength to act always in a righteous manner.

MY PRAYER FOR THE PRESIDENT

★ ★ ★

_____

_____

_____

_____

_____

_____

_____

_____

"Have I not commanded you? Be strong and of good
courage; do not be afraid, nor be dismayed,
for the LORD your God is with you wherever you go."

—JOSHUA 1:9

How have you seen prayers for our President and nation answered?

★ ★ ★

_____

_____

_____

_____

_____

_____

_____

> *This is an unprecedented time in the landmarks of our national history. Let it be known we are a nation of faith and prayer.*
>
> —REV. HURON CLAUS

The President listens to key advisors. Please pray for them too.

★ ★ ★

National Security Advisor

_____

_____

_____

_____

DEAR LORD,

Thank You for making this such a land of opportunity. But we acknowledge
that opportunities rarely come easily; someone has to plan and
construct a door of opportunity before it can be opened. Please guide our
leaders in developing policies that encourage the building of more
and more godly possibilities.

MY PRAYER FOR THE PRESIDENT

★ ★ ★

Ask, and it will be given to you; seek, and you will find;

knock, and it will be opened to you.

For everyone who asks receives, and he who seeks finds,

and to him who knocks it will be opened.

—MATTHEW 7:7—8

How have you seen prayers for our President and nation answered?

★ ★ ★

God looks not at the elegancy of your prayers, to see how neat they are; nor yet at the geometry of your prayers, to see how long they are; nor yet at the arithmetic of your prayers, to see how many they are; nor yet at the music of your prayers, not yet at the sweetness of your voice, nor yet at the logic of your prayers; but at the sincerity of your prayers, how hearty they are. There is no prayer acknowledged, approved, accepted, recorded, or rewarded by God, but that wherein the heart is sincerely and wholly.

—Thomas Brooks

The President listens to key advisors. Please pray for them too.

★ ★ ★

Director of Management & Budget

DEAR LORD,

Our government is built on the idea that people can
cooperate to find the best solutions. You are the ultimate Source of all unity,
and today we ask You: please let Your Spirit rest in extra measure
on our earthly leaders.

MY PRAYER FOR THE PRESIDENT

★ ★ ★

Yes, the LORD will give what is good;

And our land will yield its increase.

Righteousness will go before Him,

And shall make His footsteps our pathway.

—PSALM 85:12–13

HOW HAVE YOU SEEN PRAYERS FOR OUR PRESIDENT AND NATION ANSWERED?

★ ★ ★

_____

_____

_____

_____

Those people who will not be governed
by God will be ruled by tyrants.

—WILLIAM PENN

_____

_____

_____

THE PRESIDENT LISTENS TO KEY ADVISORS. PLEASE PRAY FOR THEM TOO.

★ ★ ★

CHAIRMAN OF THE JOINT CHIEFS OF STAFF

_____

_____

_____

_____

DEAR LORD,

So many times I want to go my own way, but the roads I choose are not necessarily the best ones. Thank You for the ways you nudge me back on track. Today, I acknowledge that our leaders don't always lead as You will, so I surrender them to You. Guide them back to the path of righteousness when they stray. Bring our nation's policies in line with Your desires.

MY PRAYER FOR THE PRESIDENT

★ ★ ★

_____

_____

_____

_____

_____

_____

_____

"The hand of our God is upon all those for good who seek Him, but His power and His wrath are against all those who forsake Him." So we fasted and entreated our God for this, and He answered our prayer.

—EZRA 8:22–23

HOW HAVE YOU SEEN PRAYERS FOR OUR PRESIDENT AND NATION ANSWERED?

★ ★ ★

_____

_____

_____

_____

Character is what you are in the dark.

—DWIGHT L. MOODY

_____

_____

THE PRESIDENT LISTENS TO KEY ADVISORS. PLEASE PRAY FOR THEM TOO.

★ ★ ★

SECRETARY OF TRANSPORTATION

_____

_____

_____

_____

We the People

DEAR LORD,

Protect us by Your mighty hand. Be our strong tower.

Remind us and our leaders that as individuals and as a collective nation,

we must daily put on the armor of God.

MY PRAYER FOR THE PRESIDENT

★ ★ ★

Put on the whole armor of God, that you may be able

to stand against the wiles of the devil. For we do not

wrestle against flesh and blood, but against principalities,

against powers, against the rulers of the darkness of this

age, against spiritual hosts of wickedness in the heavenly

places . . . Stand therefore, having girded your waist

with truth, having put on the breastplate of righteousness,

and having shod your feet with the preparation of the

gospel of peace; above all, taking the shield of faith

with which you will be able

to quench all the fiery darts of the wicked one.

And take the helmet of salvation, and the sword of the

Spirit, which is the word of God.

—EPHESIANS 6:11—17

How have you seen prayers for our President and nation answered?

★ ★ ★

Those who expect to reap the blessings of freedom must, like men, undergo the fatigue of supporting it.

—THOMAS PAINE

The President listens to key advisors. Please pray for them too.

★ ★ ★

SECRETARY OF DEFENSE

DEAR LORD,

I always look forward to coming home after a tiring day. Home is
a place of refuge and peace, or at least it should be.
Please guide our leaders as they consider all policies that affect our homes—
from taxes and services to safety and financing.

MY PRAYER FOR THE PRESIDENT

★ ★ ★

Continue earnestly in prayer, being vigilant in it with

thanksgiving, meanwhile praying also for us,

that God would open to us a door for the word.

—COLOSSIANS 4:2-3

How have you seen prayers for our President and nation answered?

It is not faith in the amount of praying we do, faith in our ability to pray long, beautiful, and scripturally accurate prayers, or even faith in the prayers themselves. It is faith in God—faith in who He is and faith that He rewards His children who seek Him in prayer.

—Evelyn Christensen

The President listens to key advisors. Please pray for them too.

★ ★ ★

Secretary of Housing & Urban Development

We the People

DEAR LORD,

So many of the things I own were made in other countries, and I know that many people in my community depend on selling their products and services to people overseas. Help our President and other leaders to build and maintain good trade relationships with our global neighbors.

MY PRAYER FOR THE PRESIDENT

★ ★ ★

_____

_____

_____

_____

_____

_____

_____

_____

What does the LORD require of you but to do justly,

to love mercy, and to walk humbly with your God?

—MICAH 6:8

How have you seen prayers for our President and nation answered?

> *God is at work in response to our prayers,*
> *whether we see something happening or not. If we are*
> *truly praying, "Thy will be done," forces are at work*
> *beyond our comprehension—and often, beyond our*
> *vision. But they are working just the same.*
>
> —DAVID JEREMIAH

The President listens to key advisors. Please pray for them too.

U.S. Trade Representative

DEAR LORD,

Today as I pray for my President, I ask that You also bless the leaders
of other countries. May they make wise decisions for their people. May they
seek You above all else. May their policies clear the way for Your
life-changing truth to come into every household on earth.

MY PRAYER FOR THE PRESIDENT

★ ★ ★

And Jesus came and spoke to them, saying, "All
authority has been given to Me in heaven and on earth.
Go therefore and make disciples of all the nations,
baptizing them in the name of the Father and of the
Son and of the Holy Spirit, teaching them to observe all
things that I have commanded you; and lo, I am with
you always, even to the end of the age." Amen.

—MATTHEW 28:18—20

How have you seen prayers for our President and nation answered?

★ ★ ★

_____

_____

_____

_____

_____

> *The strength of a country is the*
> *strength of its religious convictions.*
> —PRESIDENT CALVIN COOLIDGE

_____

_____

The President listens to key advisors. Please pray for them too.

★ ★ ★

U. S. Representative to the United Nations

_____

_____

_____

_____

We the People

DEAR LORD,

When You were here on earth in the person of Jesus, You ran a business,
You supported Your family, You paid taxes, and You did all of those
things under an oppressive government. Today we work and live in a nation that
enjoys great prosperity. Please help our leaders make decisions that
foster continued growth and opportunity for all people.

MY PRAYER FOR THE PRESIDENT

★ ★ ★

And we urge you, brethren, to recognize

those who labor among you, and are over you

in the Lord and admonish you, and to esteem them

very highly in love for their work's sake.

Be at peace among yourselves.

—1 THESSALONIANS 5:12-13

HOW HAVE YOU SEEN PRAYERS FOR OUR PRESIDENT AND NATION ANSWERED?

★ ★ ★

I am much indebted to the good Christian people of the country for their constant prayers and consolations; and to no one of them, more than yourself.

—PRESIDENT ABRAHAM LINCOLN

THE PRESIDENT LISTENS TO KEY ADVISORS. PLEASE PRAY FOR THEM TOO.

★ ★ ★

SECRETARY OF COMMERCE

DEAR LORD,

You offer purpose and direction for every one of us. There is no "plan B" for another person to fulfill my destiny, or the destiny of anyone else. Please help our leaders to be faithful to the roles in which You have placed them. Keep their hearts humble and their motives pure.

MY PRAYER FOR THE PRESIDENT

★ ★ ★

_____

_____

_____

_____

_____

_____

_____

_____

Trust in the LORD with all your heart, and lean not

on your own understanding; in all your ways

acknowledge Him, and He shall direct your paths.

—PROVERBS 3:5–6

How have you seen prayers for our President and nation answered?

★ ★ ★

_____

_____

_____

_____

_____

_____

_____

_____

I believe with all my heart that standing up for America means standing up for the God who has so blessed our land. We need God's help to guide our nation through stormy seas. But we can't expect Him to protect America in a crisis if we just leave Him over on the shelf in our day-to-day living.

—President Ronald Reagan

The President listens to key advisors. Please pray for them too.

★ ★ ★

The Vice President

_____

_____

_____

_____

DEAR LORD,

Surround our leaders with godly, wise advisors.

Help all of them to develop servant hearts like Yours as they serve and

lead this nation and the world.

MY PRAYER FOR THE PRESIDENT

★ ★ ★

The nations shall see and be ashamed of all their might;

They shall put their hand over their mouth;

Their ears shall be deaf.

—MICAH 7:16

How have you seen prayers for our President and nation answered?

A satisfying prayer life elevates and purifies every act of body and mind and integrates the entire personality into a single spiritual unit. In the long pull we pray only as well as we live.

—A.W. Tozer

The President listens to key advisors. Please pray for them too.

The President's Chief of Staff

We the People

DEAR LORD,

Make each of us, especially our leaders, good stewards of the abundance
of this land. Give us an appreciation of natural wonders, and an ever—deeper
awe of the supernatural Power that created them.

MY PRAYER FOR THE PRESIDENT

★ ★ ★

Oh, give thanks to the LORD! Call upon His name;

make known His deeds among the peoples!

Sing to Him, . . . talk of all His wondrous works!

—PSALM 105:1-2

HOW HAVE YOU SEEN PRAYERS FOR OUR PRESIDENT AND NATION ANSWERED?

★ ★ ★

Pray as if everything depended on God,
and work as if everything depended upon man.

—FRANCIS J. SPELLMAN

THE PRESIDENT LISTENS TO KEY ADVISORS. PLEASE PRAY FOR THEM TOO.

★ ★ ★

ENVIRONMENTAL PROTECTION AGENCY ADMINISTRATOR

DEAR LORD,

The United States is my home. I love this nation. I understand it's not perfect,
but I pledge to keep trying to bring my portion of it more in line
with the Ultimate Perfection—You. Please help our leaders to always be vigilant
in embracing You and eliminating evil.

MY PRAYER FOR THE PRESIDENT

★ ★ ★

_____

_____

_____

_____

_____

_____

_____

God has heard me; He has attended to the voice of my

prayer. Blessed be God, who has not

turned away my prayer, nor His mercy from me!

—PSALM 66:19-20

How have you seen prayers for our President and nation answered?

God has whispered two words to me over and over; Look up . . . look up. Through that quiet voice, I'm reminded to look beyond my own little life to the Creator of the universe. Without fail, looking up brings peace to my soul.

—Lisa Beamer

The President listens to key advisors. Please pray for them too.

Secretary of Homeland Defense

We the People

DEAR LORD,

It's easy to get caught up in annual uproars about government budgets,
but when I think of how much we all owe You, I have to stop in humility.
I could pay off the whole national debt single–handedly long before I could
afford the blessings You've poured out on me. Please help our leaders
to remember that all good things come from You.

MY PRAYER FOR THE PRESIDENT

★ ★ ★

_____

_____

_____

_____

_____

_____

_____

Be anxious for nothing, but in everything by prayer and

supplication, with thanksgiving, let your requests

be made known to God; and the peace of God, which

surpasses all understanding, will guard

your hearts and minds through Christ Jesus.

—PHILIPPIANS 4:6–7

How have you seen prayers for our President and nation answered?

Whoever only speaks of God, but seldom to God,
easily leases body and soul to idols.
The Christian thus places his whole future
in jeopardy by a stunted prayer life.

—Carl F. H. Henry

The President listens to key advisors. Please pray for them too.

Director of Management & Budget

DEAR LORD,

All of us are tempted to go against the laws of the land—sometimes

in big ways, other times in little ways. Make me

a person of integrity, and make our leaders people of integrity.

MY PRAYER FOR THE PRESIDENT

★ ★ ★

"Render to Caesar the things that are Caesar's,

and to God the things that are God's."

—MARK 12:17

How have you seen prayers for our President and nation answered?

I cannot recall a day when I truly saved time by jumping into the day's work without prayer. It may have seemed so at the moment, but as the day wore on, everything seemed out of sync, and time was lost.

—David Jeremiah

The President listens to key advisors. Please pray for them too.

The Surgeon General

DEAR LORD,

Our nation thrives by trade. Other nations want what we produce,
and we want what others produce. May quality abound in all our goods and
services. May our leaders promote and exemplify excellence—both in
character and in what can be bought and sold.

MY PRAYER FOR THE PRESIDENT

★ ★ ★

_____

_____

_____

_____

_____

_____

_____

_____

Regard the prayer of Your servant and his supplication,

O LORD my God, and listen to the cry and

the prayer which Your servant is praying before You.

—2 CHRONICLES 6:19

How have you seen prayers for our President and nation answered?

★ ★ ★

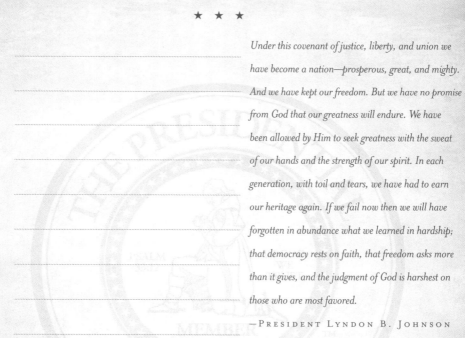

Under this covenant of justice, liberty, and union we have become a nation—prosperous, great, and mighty. And we have kept our freedom. But we have no promise from God that our greatness will endure. We have been allowed by Him to seek greatness with the sweat of our hands and the strength of our spirit. In each generation, with toil and tears, we have had to earn our heritage again. If we fail now then we will have forgotten in abundance what we learned in hardship; that democracy rests on faith, that freedom asks more than it gives, and the judgment of God is harshest on those who are most favored.

—President Lyndon B. Johnson

The President listens to key advisors. Please pray for them too.

★ ★ ★

U. S. Trade Representative

"GOD BLESS AMERICA."

We hear that phrase so often that it seems in danger of becoming trite.
Please keep our plea for Your blessing always sincere on our hearts and fresh in
Your ears. And may our leaders always remember
that the more important exhortation is "America bless God."

MY PRAYER FOR THE PRESIDENT

★ ★ ★

_Come and hear, all you who fear God, and I will
declare what He has done for my soul. God has heard
me, He has attended to the voice of my prayer._

—PSALM 66:16,19

How have you seen prayers for our President and nation answered?

_____

_____

_____

_____   *If man is man and God is God, to live without*
prayer is not merely an awful thing;
_____   *it is an infinitely foolish thing.*

—PHILLIPS BROOKS
_____

_____

The President listens to key advisors. Please pray for them too.

U. S. Supreme Court

_____

_____

_____

_____

DEAR FATHER,

As children we pray: "Now I lay me down to sleep. I pray the Lord my soul to keep." That's such a sweet offering of trust in You and in Your protection, but as adults we often fail to rely so fully on You.

Help our leaders to work intelligently for our nation's safety, but to always remember that true security is only found in You.

MY PRAYER FOR THE PRESIDENT

★ ★ ★

Who may ascend into the hill of the LORD?

Or who may stand in His holy place? He who has

clean hands and a pure heart,

he shall receive blessing from the LORD.

—PSALM 24:3–5

HOW HAVE YOU SEEN PRAYERS FOR OUR PRESIDENT
AND NATION ANSWERED?

Beyond that I only look to the gracious protection of the Divine Being whose strengthening support I humbly solicit, and whom I fervently pray to look down upon us all. May it be among the dispensations of His providence to bless our beloved country with honors and with length of days. May her ways be ways of pleasantness and all her paths be peace.

—PRESIDENT MARTIN VAN BUREN

THE PRESIDENT LISTENS TO KEY ADVISORS.
PLEASE PRAY FOR THEM TOO.

★ ★ ★

NATIONAL SECURITY ADVISOR

DEAR LORD,

Traditional wedding vows often include promises of love and fidelity
"for better or worse, richer or poorer, in sickness and in health, as long
as we both shall live." May we and our leaders all serve You with
such devotion. May our faithfulness to You bring glory to our nation.

MY PRAYER FOR THE PRESIDENT

★ ★ ★

_____

_____

_____

_____

_____

_____

Let love be without hypocrisy. Abhor what is evil.   _____

Cling to what is good. Be kindly affectionate to one   _____

another with brotherly love, in honor giving preference   _____

to one another; not lagging in diligence, fervent   _____

in spirit, serving the Lord; rejoicing in hope,   _____

patient in tribulation, continuing steadfastly in prayer.   _____

—ROMANS 12:9–12   _____

HOW HAVE YOU SEEN PRAYERS FOR OUR PRESIDENT AND NATION ANSWERED?

★ ★ ★

_____

_____

_____

_____

Prayer grows out of faithful men and women, who take hold of a vision, pray about that vision, and continually seek God in prayer. I believe that prayer changes things, and prayer can impact this country in a way that only can be done through His power.

—JOHN C. MAXWELL

THE PRESIDENT LISTENS TO KEY ADVISORS. PLEASE PRAY FOR THEM TOO.

★ ★ ★

THE FIRST FAMILY

_____

_____

_____

_____

DEAR LORD,

I don't understand all the ins and outs of politics and power, but I do know that You ultimately are in charge. Give our leaders the humility to know their limits and the passion to pursue Your desires.

MY PRAYER FOR THE PRESIDENT

★ ★ ★

_____

_____

_____

_____

_____

_____

The LORD is my rock and my fortress and my deliverer;

My God, my strength, in whom I will trust;

My shield and the horn of my salvation, my stronghold.

I will call upon the LORD, who is worthy to be praised;

So shall I be saved from my enemies.

—PSALM 18:2–3

How have you seen prayers for our President and nation answered?

Perhaps you will have to spend hours on your knees
or upon your face before the throne.
Never mind. Wait. God will do great things
to you if you will wait for Him.
Yield to Him. Cooperate with Him.

—JOHN SMITH

The President listens to key advisors. Please pray for them too.

Chairman of the Joint Chiefs of Staff

We the People

DEAR LORD,

How are we supposed to live peacefully when we share a planet with
so many billions of perspectives, needs, dreams, hurts, and individual souls that
all have sinned and fallen short of Your glory? Please let Your Spirit
guide all of us—especially our leaders—as we try to make the best of this world,
while anticipating the next one.

MY PRAYER FOR THE PRESIDENT

★ ★ ★

_____

_____

_____

_____

_____

_____

_____

Those who are wise shall shine

Like the brightness of the firmament,

And those who turn many to righteousness

Like the stars forever and ever.

—DANIEL 12:3

HOW HAVE YOU SEEN PRAYERS FOR OUR PRESIDENT
AND NATION ANSWERED?

_____

_____

_____

When I go aside in order to pray, I find my heart

unwilling to approach God; and when

_____

I tarry in prayer my heart is unwilling to abide in Him.

_____

Therefore I am compelled first to pray to God

to move my heart into Him, and when I am in Him,

_____

I pray that my heart remain in Him.

—JOHN BUNYAN

_____

THE PRESIDENT LISTENS TO KEY ADVISORS.
PLEASE PRAY FOR THEM TOO.

★ ★ ★

U. S. REPRESENTATIVE TO THE UNITED NATIONS

_____

_____

_____

_____

DEAR LORD,

You created my body as a house for the precious soul that is my being; help me to take care of this flesh appropriately. Help my leaders as their decisions affect which new foods and drugs become available. Give them wisdom in how they spend research money and how they interpret scientific information collected.

MY PRAYER FOR THE PRESIDENT

★ ★ ★

Confess your trespasses to one another, and pray for one another, that you may be healed. The effective, fervent prayer of a righteous man avails much.

—JAMES 5:16

How have you seen prayers for our President and nation answered?

★ ★ ★

_____

_____

_____

_____

Give to us, O Lord, clear vision that we may know
where to stand and what to stand for—because unless
we stand for something, we shall fall for anything.

—PETER MARSHALL

_____

_____

The President listens to key advisors. Please pray for them too.

★ ★ ★

Secretary of Agriculture

_____

_____

_____

_____

DEAR LORD,

Thank You for allowing me to live in a country where we have the luxury to spend money on trivial things. But please help our leaders to make wise decisions about when to be thrifty and when to be generous.

MY PRAYER FOR THE PRESIDENT

★ ★ ★

By this we know love, because He laid down His life

for us. And we also ought to lay down our lives for the

brethren. But whoever has this world's goods, and

sees his brother in need, and shuts up his heart

from him, how does the love of God abide in him?

—1 JOHN 3:16-17

How have you seen prayers for our President and nation answered?

★ ★ ★

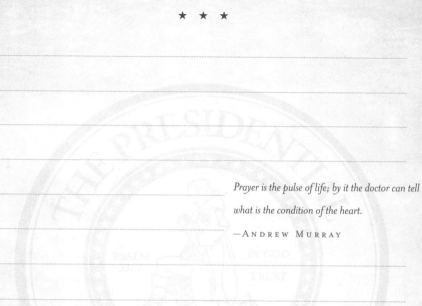

Prayer is the pulse of life; by it the doctor can tell what is the condition of the heart.

—Andrew Murray

The President listens to key advisors. Please pray for them too.

★ ★ ★

Secretary of Commerce

We the People

DEAR LORD,

Please help our leaders to know when and how our military should be used.
Please help our troops prepare for possible conflicts. Train their bodies, hearts,
and minds for service to this nation and to Your kingdom.

MY PRAYER FOR THE PRESIDENT

★ ★ ★

*Let the words of my mouth and the meditation
of my heart be acceptable in Your sight, O LORD,
my strength and my Redeemer.*

—PSALM 19:14

HOW HAVE YOU SEEN PRAYERS FOR OUR PRESIDENT AND NATION ANSWERED?

★ ★ ★

_____

_____

_____

_____

_____

_____

_____

_____

Four freedoms: The first is freedom of speech and expression—everywhere in the world. The second is freedom of everyone to worship God in his own way, everywhere in the world. The third is freedom from want . . . everywhere in the world. The fourth is freedom from fear . . . anywhere in the world.

—PRESIDENT FRANKLIN D. ROOSEVELT

THE PRESIDENT LISTENS TO KEY ADVISORS. PLEASE PRAY FOR THEM TOO.

★ ★ ★

SECRETARY OF DEFENSE

_____

_____

_____

_____

DEAR LORD,

Thank You for the ways You have prepared our leaders for their roles in the United States government. I ask that You please continue to hone their skills and intellects. Keep them alert to new realms of knowledge. And most of all, give them an unceasing desire to know You more.

MY PRAYER FOR THE PRESIDENT

★ ★ ★

Do not be wise in your own eyes; fear the LORD and depart from evil. It will be health to your flesh, and strength to your bones.

PROVERBS 3:7-8

HOW HAVE YOU SEEN PRAYERS FOR OUR PRESIDENT AND NATION ANSWERED?

★ ★ ★

Prayer is always affected by the character and conduct of him who prays. Water cannot rise above its own level, and the spotless prayer cannot flow from the spotted heart. Straight praying is never born of crooked conduct.

—LEONARD RAVENHILL

THE PRESIDENT LISTENS TO KEY ADVISORS. PLEASE PRAY FOR THEM TOO.

★ ★ ★

SECRETARY OF EDUCATION

DEAR LORD,

You are the Light of the world. May our leaders' lives
and decisions reflect Your glory. May they draw all their strength
and power from You.

MY PRAYER FOR THE PRESIDENT

★ ★ ★

I will bring the blind by a way they did not know;

I will lead them in paths they have not known.

I will make darkness light before them,

And crooked places straight.

These things I will do for them,

And not forsake them.

—ISAIAH 42:16

HOW HAVE YOU SEEN PRAYERS FOR OUR PRESIDENT AND NATION ANSWERED?

★ ★ ★

_____

_____

_____

_____

We must bring the presence of God into our families.

How do we do that? By praying.

—MOTHER TERESA

_____

_____

THE PRESIDENT LISTENS TO KEY ADVISORS. PLEASE PRAY FOR THEM TOO.

★ ★ ★

SECRETARY OF ENERGY

_____

_____

_____

_____

DEAR FATHER,

While You were here in the person of Jesus, You devoted much
of Your time to taking care of people in need. Please give our leaders wisdom in
serving others, and please use my hands and heart to help, too.

MY PRAYER FOR THE PRESIDENT

★ ★ ★

He who is mighty has done great things for me, and

holy is His name. And His mercy is on those who fear

Him from generation to generation.

—LUKE 1:49-50

HOW HAVE YOU SEEN PRAYERS FOR OUR PRESIDENT AND NATION ANSWERED?

_____
_____
_____
_____

> *When you call God "Father," you are saying*
> *there is One in heaven who hears, knows, understands,*
> *cares. Whatever a good father on earth*
> *would do for his children, that's*
> *what God in heaven will do for His children.*
> —RAY PRITCHARD

_____

THE PRESIDENT LISTENS TO KEY ADVISORS. PLEASE PRAY FOR THEM TOO.

★ ★ ★

SECRETARY OF HEALTH & HUMAN SERVICES

_____
_____
_____
_____

DEAR LORD,

As our communities grow and change, please give our leaders special
insight into how to develop the best possible living opportunities for all people.
May our neighborhoods be safe, clean, and filled with Your peace.

MY PRAYER FOR THE PRESIDENT

★ ★ ★

I will sing to the LORD as long as I live;

I will sing praise to my God while I have my being.

May my meditation be sweet

to Him, I will be glad in the LORD.

—PSALM 104:33—34

How have you seen prayers for our President and nation answered?

★ ★ ★

To men who think praying their main business . . .
does God commit the keys of His kingdom, and by them
does He work Hs spiritual wonders in this world.

—E. M. Bounds

The President listens to key advisors. Please pray for them too.

★ ★ ★

Secretary of Housing & Urban Development

DEAR LORD,

Thank You for the natural treasures You have placed in this nation.
Help us to enjoy them and use them wisely. Remind our leaders that You created
us to live in a garden. Make our leaders properly value resources
like oil and coal, which once mined cannot be replenished. Give us more
insight into recycling and conservation.

MY PRAYER FOR THE PRESIDENT

★ ★ ★

O LORD, how manifold are Your works!

In wisdom You have made them all.

The earth is full of Your possessions.

—PSALM 104:24

HOW HAVE YOU SEEN PRAYERS FOR OUR PRESIDENT
AND NATION ANSWERED?

One flag, one land, one heart, one hand,

one nation, evermore!

—OLIVER WENDELL HOLMES

THE PRESIDENT LISTENS TO KEY ADVISORS.
PLEASE PRAY FOR THEM TOO.

★ ★ ★

SECRETARY OF INTERIOR

DEAR LORD,

You made us to proclaim Your glory, but here on earth too many of us

choose to wallow in selfishness and sin. Restore the purity of our souls, Father.

Bring us back into Your communion. Help our leaders

learn the difference between rights and righteousness—both are good,

but one is infinitely better.

MY PRAYER FOR THE PRESIDENT

★ ★ ★

Wait on the LORD, and keep His way,

and He shall exalt you to inherit the land.

—PSALM 37:34

How have you seen prayers for our President and nation answered?

★ ★ ★

_____

_____

_____

_____

Let us learn together and laugh together and work
together and pray together, confident that
in the end we will triumph together in the right.

—President Jimmy Carter

_____

_____

The President listens to key advisors. Please pray for them too.

★ ★ ★

U. S. Attorney General

_____

_____

_____

_____

DEAR LORD,

We are the work of Your hands. You designed each of us to be perfect, just as You are perfect. But our sins have damaged us in every way. If Your perfect work can be marred by evil, how much more vulnerable are our own efforts? Please put Your holy hedge of protection around our leaders as they endeavor to guide us here on earth. Make their plans prosper as long as they're in Your will.

MY PRAYER FOR THE PRESIDENT

★ ★ ★

_____

_____

_____

_____

_____

_____

_____

Commit your way to the LORD, trust also

in Him, and He shall bring it to pass. _____

He shall bring forth your righteousness as the light,

and your justice as the noonday. _____

—PSALM 37:5-6

_____

HOW HAVE YOU SEEN PRAYERS FOR OUR PRESIDENT AND NATION ANSWERED?

★ ★ ★

"What Thou wilt. When Thou wilt.
How Thou wilt." I would rather speak these
three sentences from my heart in my mother tongue
than be master of all the languages in Europe.

—JOHN NEWTON

THE PRESIDENT LISTENS TO KEY ADVISORS. PLEASE PRAY FOR THEM TOO.

★ ★ ★

SECRETARY OF LABOR

DEAR LORD,

In the United States we choose our leaders. This is a tremendous privilege and responsibility. Please help us to take elections seriously. Guide us to know the best candidates. Prompt us if You desire us to seek public office ourselves. And above all, help us to support our leaders as You would have us do, no matter who wins.

MY PRAYER FOR THE PRESIDENT

★ ★ ★

Remind them to be subject to rulers and authorities, to obey, to be ready for every good work, to speak evil of no one, to be peaceable, gentle, showing all humility to all men.

—TITUS 3:1–2

How have you seen prayers for our President and nation answered?

★ ★ ★

_____

_____

_____

_____

_____

_____

_____

_____

*If you really want to fight evil, find out
a way to contribute your time and efforts and money
and talent to making one person's life brighter.
That's how we change America. I like to say, each of us
can't do everything, but each of us can do one thing.
America changes one heart, one soul,
one conscience at a time.*

—President George W. Bush

The President listens to key advisors. Please pray for them too.

★ ★ ★

Secretary of State

_____

_____

_____

_____

DEAR LORD,

So many people come to this country to pursue endless horizons of opportunities. Please help our leaders be wise in helping us all achieve our dreams. And may all our dreams be faithful to You.

MY PRAYER FOR THE PRESIDENT

★ ★ ★

Blessed be the name of the LORD from this time

forth and forevermore! From the rising of the sun to its

going down the LORD'S name is to be praised.

—PSALM 113:2-3

HOW HAVE YOU SEEN PRAYERS FOR OUR PRESIDENT
AND NATION ANSWERED?

★ ★ ★

_____

_____

_____

_____

_____

I remember my mother's prayers and they have always

followed me. They have clung to me all my life.

—PRESIDENT ABRAHAM LINCOLN

_____

THE PRESIDENT LISTENS TO KEY ADVISORS.
PLEASE PRAY FOR THEM TOO.

★ ★ ★

THE SURGEON GENERAL

_____

_____

_____

_____

DEAR LORD,

I've heard that the best way to know what's important to someone
is to see what they do with their money. Father, when people look at what our
nation spends, may they see Your desires in action. Prompt our President
and other leaders to follow Your priorities.

MY PRAYER FOR THE PRESIDENT

★ ★ ★

_____

_____

_____

_____

_____

_____

_____

_____

If you abide in Me, and My words   _____

abide in you, you will ask what you desire,   _____

and it shall be done for you.   _____

—JOHN 15:7   _____

HOW HAVE YOU SEEN PRAYERS FOR OUR PRESIDENT
AND NATION ANSWERED?

★ ★ ★

_____

_____

_____

_____

_____

Let not the foundation of our hope rest upon man's
wisdom. It must be felt that there is no national security
but in the nation's humble, acknowledged dependence
upon God and His over ruling Providence.

—PRESIDENT FRANKLIN PIERCE

_____

THE PRESIDENT LISTENS TO KEY ADVISORS.
PLEASE PRAY FOR THEM TOO.

★ ★ ★

SECRETARY OF TREASURY

_____

_____

_____

_____

DEAR LORD,

The people of the United States have been so very blessed,
but many also understand great sacrifice. May our leaders honor those who
have sacrificed for this country, and may we all be ready to place
everything on the altar for You.

MY PRAYER FOR THE PRESIDENT

★ ★ ★

_____

_____

_____

_____

_____

_____

With Him are wisdom and strength,

He has counsel and understanding. . . .

He makes nations great, and destroys them;

He enlarges nations, and guides them.

—JOB 12:13, 23

HOW HAVE YOU SEEN PRAYERS FOR OUR PRESIDENT
AND NATION ANSWERED?

_Entering thus solemnly into covenant
with each other, may we reverently invoke and
confidently expect the favor and help of Almighty
God—that He will give to me wisdom, strength, and
fidelity, and to our people a spirit of fraternity
and love of righteousness and peace._

—PRESIDENT BENJAMIN HARRISON

THE PRESIDENT LISTENS TO KEY ADVISORS.
PLEASE PRAY FOR THEM TOO.

★ ★ ★

SECRETARY OF VETERANS AFFAIRS

DEAR LORD,

Today I just pray for the President. So much hope, fear, support,

anger, respect, and ridicule are focused on this one person. So many demands

for attention. So much confusion to untangle. Father, give our President

supernatural wisdom and strength for all the rigors of the day.

May our President dream of You tonight, then awaken fully refreshed

and ready to do Your will.

MY PRAYER FOR THE PRESIDENT

★ ★ ★

You shall not revile God,

nor curse a ruler of your people.

—EXODUS 22:28

HOW HAVE YOU SEEN PRAYERS FOR OUR PRESIDENT AND NATION ANSWERED?

★ ★ ★

_____

_____

_____

_____

From my mother I learned the value
of prayer, how to have dreams and believe
I could make them come true.

—PRESIDENT RONALD REAGAN

_____

THE PRESIDENT LISTENS TO KEY ADVISORS. PLEASE PRAY FOR THEM TOO.

★ ★ ★

THE FIRST FAMILY

_____

_____

_____

_____

DEAR LORD,

Someday You will sit in judgment on all this earth, and only the mercy

of Your Son will save us from Your righteous condemnation.

Lord, make us living witnesses of that mercy. May our leaders be people

who also know and love Jesus.

MY PRAYER FOR THE PRESIDENT

★ ★ ★

The things that are impossible with men

are possible with God.

—LUKE 18:27

HOW HAVE YOU SEEN PRAYERS FOR OUR PRESIDENT AND NATION ANSWERED?

God loves America. When you consider what He went through to bring our forbearers to this magnificent land, and when you realize what He accomplished in bringing forth a new nation on this continent—a government founded on Christian principles and dedicated to life, liberty, and the pursuit of happiness—you have to realize that He had a dramatic vision and purpose for this nation.

—D. JAMES KENNEDY

THE PRESIDENT LISTENS TO KEY ADVISORS. PLEASE PRAY FOR THEM TOO.

U. S. SUPREME COURT

DEAR LORD,

Today I plead for the children growing up in this hyper—competitive world.

Help our leaders make sure the necessary lessons come to every child.

May our children learn in secure, encouraging environments. May our teachers

be given the appropriate tools, training, and support from all levels—

parents, administrators, and public officials.

MY PRAYER FOR THE PRESIDENT

★ ★ ★

Now this is the confidence that we have in Him,

that if we ask anything according to His will,

He hears us. And if we know that He hears us, what—

ever we ask, we know that we have the petitions

that we have asked of Him.

—1 JOHN 5:14-15

How have you seen prayers for our President and nation answered?

Though we cling to the principle that church and state should be separate, we do not purpose to separate man from God.

—MELVIN LAIRD

The President listens to key advisors. Please pray for them too.

Secretary of Education

DEAR LORD,

Thank You for giving us a heritage of religious freedom, but I know
that liberty did not originate with the First Amendment, or even with the
Pilgrims. Religious freedom originated with You—You let us each one of us elect
whether we want life in You or death in self. Help our leaders
to acknowledge this truth every day.

MY PRAYER FOR THE PRESIDENT

★ ★ ★

I thank God, whom I serve with a pure conscience,

as my forefathers did, as without ceasing

I remember you in my prayers night and day.

—2 TIMOTHY 1:3

How have you seen prayers for our President and nation answered?

★ ★ ★

_____

_____

_____

_____

_____

_____

It cannot be emphasized too strongly or too often that this great nation was founded, not by religionists, but by Christians; not on religions, but on the gospel of Jesus Christ. For this very reason peoples of other faiths have been afforded asylum, prosperity, and freedom of worship here.

—Patrick Henry

The President listens to key advisors. Please pray for them too.

★ ★ ★

U. S. Attorney General

_____

_____

_____

_____

DEAR LORD,

Sometimes I just have to stop; I'm empty, exhausted, fried. I can only imagine what my leaders go through with their extra burdens. Please grant them renewed energy. Refresh their minds. Rejuvenate their bodies. Restore their souls. Do it all to Your glory and to the benefit of this nation.

MY PRAYER FOR THE PRESIDENT

★ ★ ★

_____

_____

_____

_____

_____

_____

The LORD is my shepherd; I shall not want.

He makes me to lie down in green pastures; He leads

me beside the still waters. He restores my soul.

He leads me in the paths of righteousness

For His name's sake.

—PSALM 23:1–3

HOW HAVE YOU SEEN PRAYERS FOR OUR PRESIDENT
AND NATION ANSWERED?

★ ★ ★

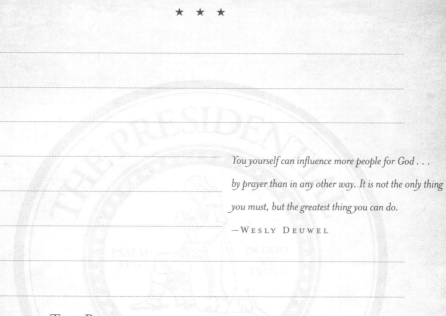

*You yourself can influence more people for God . . .
by prayer than in any other way. It is not the only thing
you must, but the greatest thing you can do.*

—WESLY DEUWEL

THE PRESIDENT LISTENS TO KEY ADVISORS.
PLEASE PRAY FOR THEM TOO.

★ ★ ★

WHITE HOUSE CHIEF OF STAFF

DEAR FATHER,

The first steps we take as toddlers are into a parent's loving arms.
We soon dash there for safety, for comfort, for rest, and for myriad other
reasons. May our leaders—especially the President—all run to You today.
The rest of us are only safe when our leaders are in Your arms.

MY PRAYER FOR THE PRESIDENT

★ ★ ★

_____

_____

_____

_____

_____

_____

_____

_____

Call upon me in the day of trouble; I will deliver

you, and you shall glorify Me.

—PSALM 50:15

How have you seen prayers for our President and nation answered?

★ ★ ★

_God grants liberty only to those who love it, and are
always ready to guard and defend it._

—Daniel Webster

The President listens to key advisors. Please pray for them too.

★ ★ ★

Secretary of Defense

DEAR LORD,

"Follow the leader" is far more than a child's game. It's life—and—death serious. Make us good followers, and make our leaders great. And may You be proclaimed publicly as both our ultimate Leader and eternal destination. Thank You for seeing us through the journey.

MY PRAYER FOR THE PRESIDENT

★ ★ ★

For I know the thoughts that I think toward you, says the LORD, thoughts of peace and not of evil, to give you a future and a hope. Then you will call upon Me and go and pray to Me, and I will listen to you. And you will seek Me and find Me, when you search for Me with all your heart.

—JEREMIAH 29:11—13

How have you seen prayers for our President and nation answered?

Pray for great things, expect great things, work for great things, but above all, pray.

—R. A. Torrey

The President listens to key advisors. Please pray for them too.

The Vice President

Days to Keep in Prayer

★ ★ ★

Federal Holidays

★ ★ ★

New Year's Day . . . . January 1

Martin Luther King, Jr., Day . . . . . . Third Monday in January

Presidents Day . . . . Third Monday in February

Memorial Day . . . . Final Monday in May

Independence Day . . . . July 4

Labor Day . . . . First Monday in September

Columbus Day . . . . Second Monday in October

Veterans Day . . . . November 11

Thanksgiving Day . . . . Fourth Thursday in November

Christmas Day . . . . December 25

National Observances

★ ★ ★

National Day of Prayer . . . . First Thursday in May

Mother's Day . . . . Second Sunday in May

Father's Day . . . . Third Sunday in June

Juneteenth (Liberation of Slaves) . . . . . June 19

Grandparents' Day . . . . Sunday after Labor Day

Patriot Day . . . . September 11

Citizenship or Constitution Day . . . . September 17

National Children's Day . . . . Second Sunday in October

Please check www.presidentialprayerteam.org for updates about other times of urgent prayer, and be observant for information about local and national elections that also need to be covered in prayer.

THE PRESIDENT'S KEY ADVISORS

The President depends on information and advice from
other people, especially those who fill the roles listed on the following pages.
For more information on the issues and responsibilities these people face,
please see the role–specific websites listed.

★ ★ ★

THE CABINET

Secretary of Agriculture

www.usda.gov

Secretary of Commerce

www.doc.gov

Secretary of Defense

www.dod.gov

Secretary of Education

www.ed.gov

Secretary of Energy

www.energy.gov

Secretary of Health
& Human Services

www.dhhs.gov

Secretary of Homeland Security

www.whitehouse.gov/homeland/

Secretary of Housing &
Urban Development

www.hud.gov

Secretary of Interior

www.doi.gov

U. S. Attorney General
(Department of Justice)

www.usdoj.gov

Secretary of Labor	Secretary of Treasury
www.dol.gov	www.ustreas.gov
Secretary of State	Secretary of Veterans Affairs
www.state.gov	www.va.gov
Secretary of Transportation	
www.dot.gov	

CABINET–RANK MEMBERS

★ ★ ★

The Vice President	Director of Management & Budget
www.whitehouse.gov/vicepresident/	www.omb.gov
White House Chief of Staff	Director of National Drug Control Policy
	www.whitehousedrugpolicy.gov
Environmental Protection Agency Administrator	U. S. Trade Representative
www.epa.gov	www.ustr.gov

THE PRESIDENT'S KEY ADVISORS

★ ★ ★

OTHER LEADERS

★ ★ ★

Chairman of the
Joint Chiefs of Staff

U. S. House of Representatives

---

www.dtic.mil/jcs/

The First Family

www.house.gov

U. S. Senate

---

www.whitehouse.gov

National Security Advisor

www.senate.gov

U. S. Supreme Court

---

www.whitehouse.gov/nsc/

U. S. Representative
to the United Nations

www.supremecourtus.gov

Surgeon General

---

www.un.int/usa/

www.surgeongeneral.gov

When the righteous are in authority, the people rejoice; But when a wicked man rules, the people groan.

—Proverbs 29:2

Let every soul be subject to the governing authorities. For there is no authority except from God, and the authorities that exist are appointed by God. Therefore whoever resists the authority resists the ordinance of God, and those who resist will bring judgment on themselves. For rulers are not a terror to good works, but to evil. Do you want to be unafraid of the authority? Do what is good, and you will have praise from the same. For he is God's minister to you for good. But if you do evil, be afraid; for he does not bear the sword in vain; for he is God's minister, an avenger to execute wrath on him who practices evil. Therefore you must be subject, not only because of wrath but also for conscience' sake. For because of this you also pay taxes, for they are God's ministers attending continually to this very thing. Render therefore to all their due: taxes to whom taxes are due, customs to whom customs, fear to whom fear, honor to whom honor.

—Romans 13:1–7

Therefore I exhort first of all that supplications, prayers, intercessions, and giving of thanks be made for all men, for kings and all who are in authority, that we may lead a quiet and peaceable life in all godliness and reverence. For this is good and acceptable in the sight of God our Savior, who desires all men to be saved and to come to the knowledge of the truth.

—1 Timothy 2:1–4

"Well done, good and faithful servant; you have been faithful over a few things, I will make you ruler over many things. Enter into the joy of your lord."

—Matthew 25:23

So when He had washed their feet, taken His garments, and sat down again, He said to them, "Do you know what I have done to you? You call Me Teacher and Lord, and you say well, for so I am. If I then, your Lord and Teacher, have washed your feet, you also ought to wash one another's feet. For I have given you an example, that you should do as I have done to you."

—John 13:12–15

Scriptures about Leaders & Leadership

★ ★ ★

LORD, who may abide in Your
  tabernacle?
Who may dwell in Your holy hill?
He who walks uprightly,
And works righteousness,
And speaks the truth in his heart;
He who does not backbite with his
  tongue,
Nor does evil to his neighbor,
Nor does he take up a reproach
  against his friend;
In whose eyes a vile person is despised,
But he honors those who fear the
  LORD;
He who swears to his own hurt and
  does not change;
He who does not put out his money at
  usury,
Nor does he take a bribe against the
  innocent.
He who does these things shall never
  be moved.
                 —PSALM 15

Then Deborah and Barak the son of
  Abinoam sang on that day, saying:
"When leaders lead in Israel,
When the people willingly offer
  themselves,
Bless the LORD!
Hear, O kings! Give ear, O princes!
I, even I, will sing to the LORD;
I will sing praise to the LORD God of
  Israel."
              —JUDGES 5:1–3

It is better to trust in the LORD
Than to put confidence in man.
It is better to trust in the LORD
Than to put confidence in princes.
            —PSALM 118:8–19

It was not you who sent me here,
but God; and He has made me a
father to Pharaoh, and lord of all his
house, and a ruler throughout all the
land of Egypt.
            —GENESIS 45:8

Listen now to my voice; I will give
you counsel, and God will be with you:
Stand before God for the people, so
that you may bring the difficulties to
God. And you shall teach them the
statutes and the laws, and show them
the way in which they must walk and the
work they must do. Moreover you shall
select from all the people able men,
such as fear God, men of truth, hating
covetousness; and place such over them
to be rulers . . . So it will be easier for
you, for they will bear the burden with
you. If you do this thing, and God so
commands you, then you will be able to
endure, and all this people will also go
to their place in peace.
           —EXODUS 18:19–23

★ ★ ★

The righteous should choose his
friends carefully,
For the way of the wicked leads them
astray.
—PROVERBS 12:26

Without counsel, plans go awry,
But in the multitude of counselors
they are established.
—PROVERBS 15:22

There are many plans in a man's
heart,
Nevertheless the LORD 's counsel—that
will stand.
—PROVERBS 19:21

Plans are established by counsel;
By wise counsel wage war.
—PROVERBS 20:18

For unto us a Child is born, Unto
us a Son is given; And the government
will be upon His shoulder. And His
name will be called Wonderful,
Counselor, Mighty God, Everlasting
Father, Prince of Peace.
—ISAIAH 9:6

"Woe to the rebellious children," says
the Lord,
"Who take counsel, but not of Me,
And who devise plans, but not of My
Spirit,
That they may add sin to sin."
—ISAIAH 30:1

The earth is the LORD 's, and all its
fullness,
The world and those who dwell therein.
—PSALM 24:1

All the nations of the world will
stand amazed at what the LORD will do
for you.
—MICAH 7:16 (NLT)

But those who wait on the LORD
Shall renew their strength;
They shall mount up with wings like
eagles,
They shall run and not be weary,
They shall walk and not faint.
—ISAIAH 40:31

We had spoken to the king, saying,
"The hand of our God is upon all
those for good who seek Him, but His
power and His wrath are against all
those who forsake Him." So we fasted
and entreated our God for this, and
He answered our prayer.
—EZRA 8:22—23

Scriptures about Leaders & Leadership

★ ★ ★

Don't just pretend that you love others. Really love them. Hate what is wrong. Stand on the side of the good. Love each other with genuine affection, and take delight in honoring each other. Never be lazy in your work, but serve the Lord enthusiastically. Be glad for all God is planning for you. Be patient in trouble, and always be prayerful.

—ROMANS 12:9–12 (NLT)

Oh, give thanks to the LORD!
Call upon His name;
Make known His deeds among the
   peoples!
Sing to Him, sing psalms to Him;
Talk of all His wondrous works!
Glory in His holy name;
Let the hearts of those rejoice who
   seek the LORD!
Seek the LORD and His strength;
Seek His face evermore!

—PSALM 105:1–4

But without faith it is impossible to please Him, for he who comes to God must believe that He is, and that He is a rewarder of those who diligently seek Him.

—HEBREWS 11:6

Be diligent to present yourself approved to God, a worker who does not need to be ashamed, rightly dividing the word of truth.

—2 TIMOTHY 2:15

For this reason I bow my knees to the Father of our Lord Jesus Christ, from whom the whole family in heaven and earth is named, that He would grant you, according to the riches of His glory, to be strengthened with might through His Spirit in the inner man, that Christ may dwell in your hearts through faith; that you, being rooted and grounded in love, may be able to comprehend with all the saints what is the width and length and depth and height—to know the love of Christ which passes knowledge; that you may be filled with all the fullness of God.

—EPHESIANS 3:14–19

You are the light of the world. A city that is set on a hill cannot be hidden. Nor do they light a lamp and put it under a basket, but on a lampstand, and it gives light to all who are in the house. Let your light so shine before men, that they may see your good works and glorify your Father in heaven.

—MATTHEW 5:14–16

Those who are wise shall shine
Like the brightness of the firmament,
And those who turn many to
   righteousness
Like the stars forever and ever.
—DANIEL 12:3

You shall receive power when the Holy Spirit has come upon you; and you shall be witnesses to Me in Jerusalem, and in all Judea and Samaria, and to the end of the earth.
—ACTS 1:8

For God so loved the world that He gave His only begotten Son, that whoever believes in Him should not perish but have everlasting life.
—JOHN 3:16

By this we know love, because He laid down His life for us. And we also ought to lay down our lives for the brethren. But whoever has this world's goods, and sees his brother in need, and shuts up his heart from him, how does the love of God abide in him?
—1 JOHN 3:16–17

This Book of the Law shall not depart from your mouth, but you shall meditate in it day and night, that you may observe to do according to all that is written in it. For then you will make your way prosperous, and then you will have good success.
—JOSHUA 1:8

You shall remember the LORD your God, for it is He who gives you power to get wealth, that He may establish His covenant which He swore to your fathers, as it is this day.
—DEUTERONOMY 8:18

Trust in the LORD with all your heart,
And lean not on your own
   understanding;
In all your ways acknowledge Him,
And He shall direct your paths.
Do not be wise in your own eyes;
Fear the Lord and depart from evil.
It will be health to your flesh,
And strength to your bones.
Honor the LORD with your possessions,
And with the firstfruits of all your
   increase;
So your barns will be filled with plenty,
And your vats will overflow with
   new wine.
—PROVERBS 3:5–10

Scriptures about Leaders & Leadership

★ ★ ★

May the Lord be with you; and may you prosper . . . Only may the LORD give you wisdom and understanding, and give you charge . . . that you may keep the law of the LORD your God. Then you will prosper, if you take care to fulfill the statutes and judgments with which the LORD charged Moses concerning Israel. Be strong and of good courage; do not fear nor be dismayed.

—1 Chronicles 22:11–13

Now it shall come to pass, if you diligently obey the voice of the LORD your God, to observe carefully all His commandments which I command you today, that the LORD your God will set you high above all nations of the earth. And all these blessings shall come upon you and overtake you, because you obey the voice of the Lord your God . . . Then all peoples of the earth shall see that you are called by the name of the Lord, and they shall be afraid of you. And the Lord will grant you plenty of goods, in the fruit of your body, in the increase of your livestock, and in the produce of your ground, in the land of which the Lord swore to your fathers to give you. The Lord will open to you His good treasure, the heavens, to give the rain to your land in its season, and to bless all the work of your hand. You shall lend to many nations, but you shall not borrow . . . But it shall come to pass, if you do not obey the voice of the Lord your God, to observe carefully all His commandments and His statutes which I command you today, that all these curses will come upon you and overtake you . . . The Lord will send on you cursing, confusion, and rebuke in all that you set your hand to do, until you are destroyed and until you perish quickly, because of the wickedness of your doings in which you have forsaken Me.

—Deuteronomy 28:1–2, 10–12, 15, 20

Through wisdom a house is built,
And by understanding it is established;
By knowledge the rooms are filled
With all precious and pleasant riches.
A wise man is strong,
Yes, a man of knowledge increases
    strength;
For by wise counsel you will wage your
    own war,
And in a multitude of counselors
    there is safety.

—Proverbs 24:3–6

★ ★ ★

Be strong, therefore, and prove yourself a man. And keep the charge of the Lord your God: to walk in His ways, to keep His statutes, His commandments, His judgments, and His testimonies, as it is written in the Law of Moses, that you may prosper in all that you do and wherever you turn.

—1 KINGS 2:2–3

He has shown you, O man, what is
   good;
And what does the LORD require of you
But to do justly,
To love mercy,
And to walk humbly with your God?

—MICAH 6:8

Behold, how good and how pleasant it is
For brethren to dwell together in unity!

—PSALM 133:1

The God of our fathers raised up Jesus whom you murdered by hanging on a tree. Him God has exalted to His right hand to be Prince and Savior, to give repentance to Israel and forgiveness of sins. And we are His witnesses to these things, and so also is the Holy Spirit whom God has given to those who obey Him.

—ACTS 5:10–32

He who sows sparingly will also reap sparingly, and he who sows bountifully will also reap bountifully. So let each one give as he purposes in his heart, not grudgingly or of necessity; for God loves a cheerful giver. And God is able to make all grace abound toward you, that you, always having all sufficiency in all things, may have an abundance for every good work. As it is written: "He has dispersed abroad, He has given to the poor; His righteousness endures forever."

—2 CORINTHIANS 9:6–9

Set your mind on things above, not on things on the earth.

—COLOSSIANS 3:2

Whatever you do in word or deed, do all in the name of the Lord Jesus, giving thanks to God the Father through Him.

—COLOSSIANS 3:17

Lay up for yourselves treasures in heaven, where neither moth nor rust destroys and where thieves do not break in and steal. For where your treasure is, there your heart will be also.

—MATTHEW 6:20–21

★ ★ ★

Having been set free from sin, and having become slaves of God, you have your fruit to holiness, and the end, everlasting life. For the wages of sin is death, but the gift of God is eternal life in Christ Jesus our Lord.

—Romans 6:22—23

Repay no one evil for evil. Have regard for good things in the sight of all men. If it is possible, as much as depends on you, live peaceably with all men. Beloved, do not avenge yourselves, but rather give place to wrath; for it is written, "Vengeance is Mine, I will repay," says the Lord. Therefore "If your enemy is hungry, feed him; If he is thirsty, give him a drink; For in so doing you will heap coals of fire on his head." Do not be overcome by evil, but overcome evil with good.

—Romans 12:17—21

I will lead them in paths they have not known.
I will make darkness light before them,
And crooked places straight.
These things I will do for them,
And not forsake them.

—Isaiah 42:16

Do not be deceived, God is not mocked; for whatever a man sows, that he will also reap. For he who sows to his flesh will of the flesh reap corruption, but he who sows to the Spirit will of the Spirit reap everlasting life. And let us not grow weary while doing good, for in due season we shall reap if we do not lose heart. Therefore, as we have opportunity, let us do good to all, especially to those who are of the household of faith.

—Galatians 6:7—10

Let us consider one another in order to stir up love and good works.

—Hebrews 10:24

Let every man be swift to hear, slow to speak, slow to wrath; for the wrath of man does not produce the righteousness of God.

—James 1:19—20

If any of you lacks wisdom, let him ask of God, who gives to all liberally and without reproach, and it will be given to him.

—James 1:5

I will instruct you and teach you in the way you should go;
I will guide you with My eye.

—Psalm 32:8

★ ★ ★

For I know the thoughts that I think toward you, says the Lord, thoughts of peace and not of evil, to give you a future and a hope. Then you will call upon Me and go and pray to Me, and I will listen to you. And you will seek Me and find Me, when you search for Me with all your heart. I will be found by you, says the LORD.

—JEREMIAH 29:11–14

Again I say to you that if two of you agree on earth concerning anything that they ask, it will be done for them by My Father in heaven. For where two or three are gathered together in My name, I am there in the midst of them.

—MATTHEW 18:19–20

The first day that you set your heart to understand, and to humble yourself before your God, your words were heard

—DANIEL 10:12

If you abide in Me, and My words abide in you, you will ask what you desire, and it shall be done for you.

—JOHN 15:7

Be anxious for nothing, but in everything by prayer and supplication, with thanksgiving, let your requests be made known to God; and the peace of God, which surpasses all understanding, will guard your hearts and minds through Christ Jesus.

—PHILIPPIANS 4:6–7

Confess your trespasses to one another, and pray for one another, that you may be healed. The effective, fervent prayer of a righteous man avails much.

—JAMES 5:16

If My people who are called by My name will humble themselves, and pray and seek My face, and turn from their wicked ways, then I will hear from heaven, and will forgive their sin and heal their land.

—2 CHRONICLES 7:14

The sacrifice of the wicked is an
  abomination to the LORD,
But the prayer of the upright is His
  delight.

—PROVERBS 15:8

★ ★ ★

Rejoice always, pray without ceasing, in everything give thanks; for this is the will of God in Christ Jesus for you.

—1 THESSALONIANS 5:16–18

The Holy Spirit helps us in our distress. For we don't even know what we should pray for, nor how we should pray. But the Holy Spirit prays for us with groanings that cannot be expressed in words.

—ROMANS 8:26 (NLT)

The LORD is my rock and my fortress
and my deliverer;
My God, my strength, in whom I will
trust;
My shield and the horn of my salvation,
my stronghold.
I will call upon the Lord, who is worthy to be praised;
So shall I be saved from my enemies.

—PSALM 18:2–3

Hear a just cause, O LORD,
Attend to my cry;
Give ear to my prayer which is not
from deceitful lips.

—PSALM 17:1

For this reason we also, since the day we heard it, do not cease to pray for you, and to ask that you may be filled with the knowledge of His will in all wisdom and spiritual understanding; that you may walk worthy of the Lord, fully pleasing Him, being fruitful in every good work and increasing in the knowledge of God; strengthened with all might, according to His glorious power, for all patience and longsuffering with joy;

—COLOSSIANS 1:9–11

And this I pray, that your love may abound still more and more in knowledge and all discernment, that you may approve the things that are excellent, that you may be sincere and without offense till the day of Christ.

—PHILIPPIANS 1:9–10

Now to Him who is able to do exceedingly abundantly above all that we ask or think, according to the power that works in us, to Him be glory in the church by Christ Jesus to all generations, forever and ever. Amen.

—EPHESIANS 3:20–21

About the Presidential Prayer Team

★ ★ ★

After the terrorist attacks on September 11, 2001, the President of the United States asked all Americans to pray. *The Presidential Prayer Team* was launched less than a week later. Since then, millions have answered the President's call and many have joined *The Presidential Prayer Team,* receiving regular email updates on national prayer needs. Anyone can join. Membership is free. Join at www.presidential-prayerteam.org or www.presidentialprayerkids.org for children.

The Presidential Prayer Team is not affiliated with any political party or official. It gains no direction or support, official or unofficial, from the current administration, from any agency of the government or from any political party, so that it may be free and unencumbered to equally serve the prayer needs of all current and future leaders of our great nation.

The Presidential Prayer Team seeks the involvement of all Americans who are committed to pray for the President, crossing ethnic, political and religious backgrounds for the benefit of the nation. It holds no affiliation with any political or religious organizations, nor will it ever be used for political purposes.

To register your membership on *The Presidential Prayer Team* and receive a membership decal and weekly prayer updates, go to www.presidentialprayerteam.org.